DISCOVER OCTOPUSES

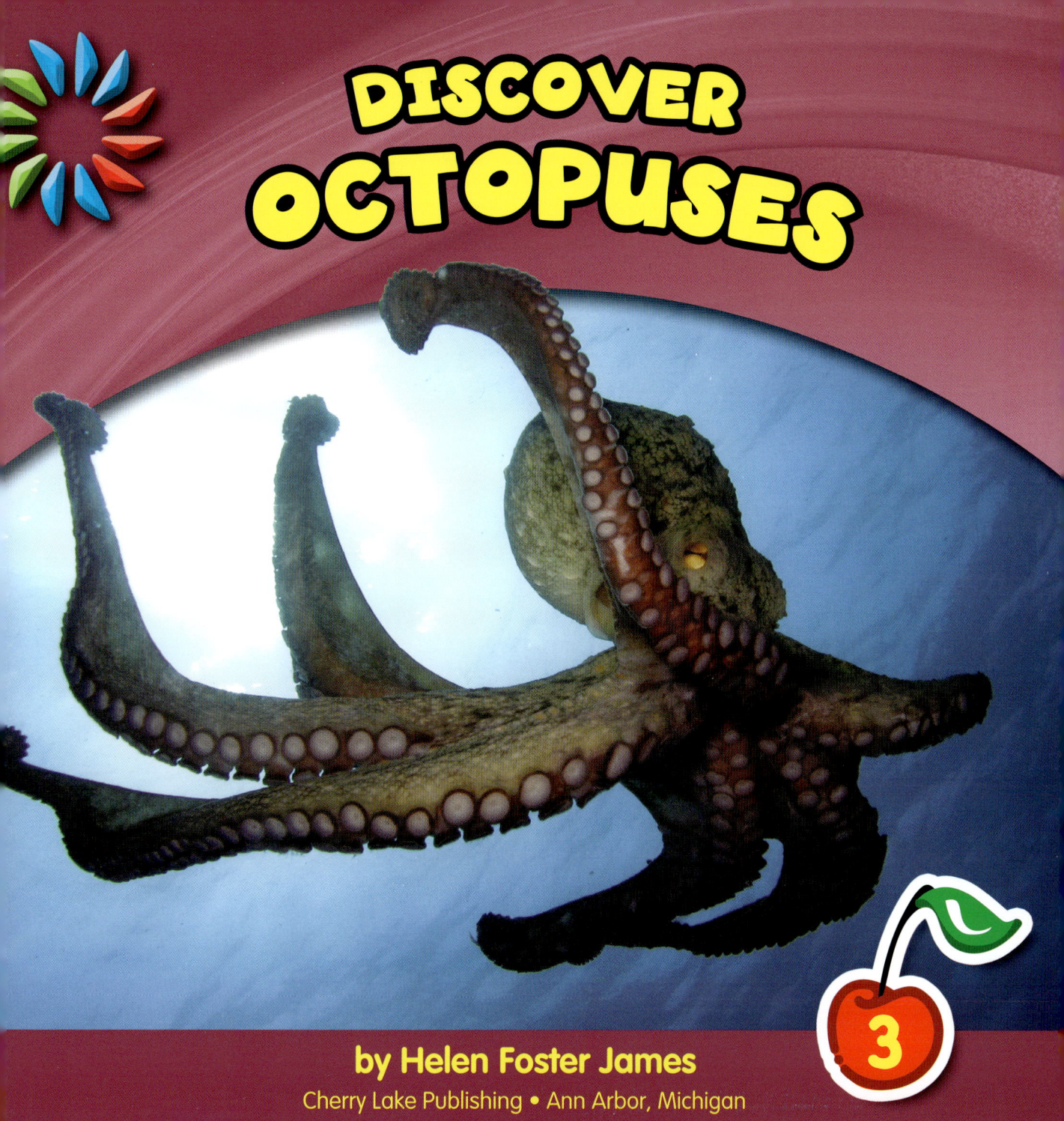

by Helen Foster James

Cherry Lake Publishing • Ann Arbor, Michigan

3

Cherry Lake Publishing

Published in the United States of America
by Cherry Lake Publishing
Ann Arbor, Michigan
www.cherrylakepublishing.com

Content Adviser: William McLellan, research associate, department of biology and marine biology, University of North Carolina, Wilmington
Reading Adviser: Marla Conn, ReadAbility, Inc

Photo Credits: © Vittorio Bruno/Shutterstock Images, cover, 12, 16; © Pinosub/Shutterstock Images, 4; © Rich Carey/Shutterstock Images, 6; © HNC Photo/Shutterstock Images, 8; © Peter Leahy/Shutterstock Images, 10; © NatalieJean/Shutterstock Images, 14; © almondd/Shutterstock Images, 18; © EcoPrint/Shutterstock Images, 20

Copyright ©2016 by Cherry Lake Publishing
All rights reserved. No part of this book may be reproduced or utilized in any form or by any means without written permission from the publisher.

Library of Congress Cataloging-in-Publication Data
James, Helen Foster, 1951-author.
  Discover octopuses / Helen Foster James.
     pages cm.—(Splash!)
  Summary: "This Level 3 guided reader introduces basic facts about octopuses, including their physical characteristics, diet, and habitat. Simple callouts ask the student to think in new ways, supporting inquiry-based reading. Additional text features and search tools, including a glossary and an index, help students locate information and learn new words—Provided by publisher.
  Audience: Ages 6–10.
  Includes bibliographical references and index.
  ISBN 978-1-63362-602-7 (hardcover)—ISBN 978-1-63362-782-6 (pdf)—ISBN 978-1-63362-692-8 (pbk.)—ISBN (invalid) 978-1-63362-872-4 (ebook)
  1. Octopuses—Juvenile literature. I. Title.

QL430.3.O2J325 2016
594.56—dc23

2015000575

Cherry Lake Publishing would like to acknowledge the work of the Partnership for 21st Century Skills. Please visit www.p21.org for more information.

Printed in the United States of America
Corporate Graphics

TABLE OF CONTENTS

- **5** So Many Arms!
- **11** Octopuses Keep Safe
- **19** Looking at Tide Pools

- 22 Think About It
- 22 Find Out More
- 23 Glossary
- 24 Index
- 24 About the Author

4

So Many Arms!

An octopus has eight **tentacles**, or arms. ***Octo*** means "eight." An octopus might lose an arm. It will grow back over time.

The name "octopus" comes from the fact that the animal has eight arms.

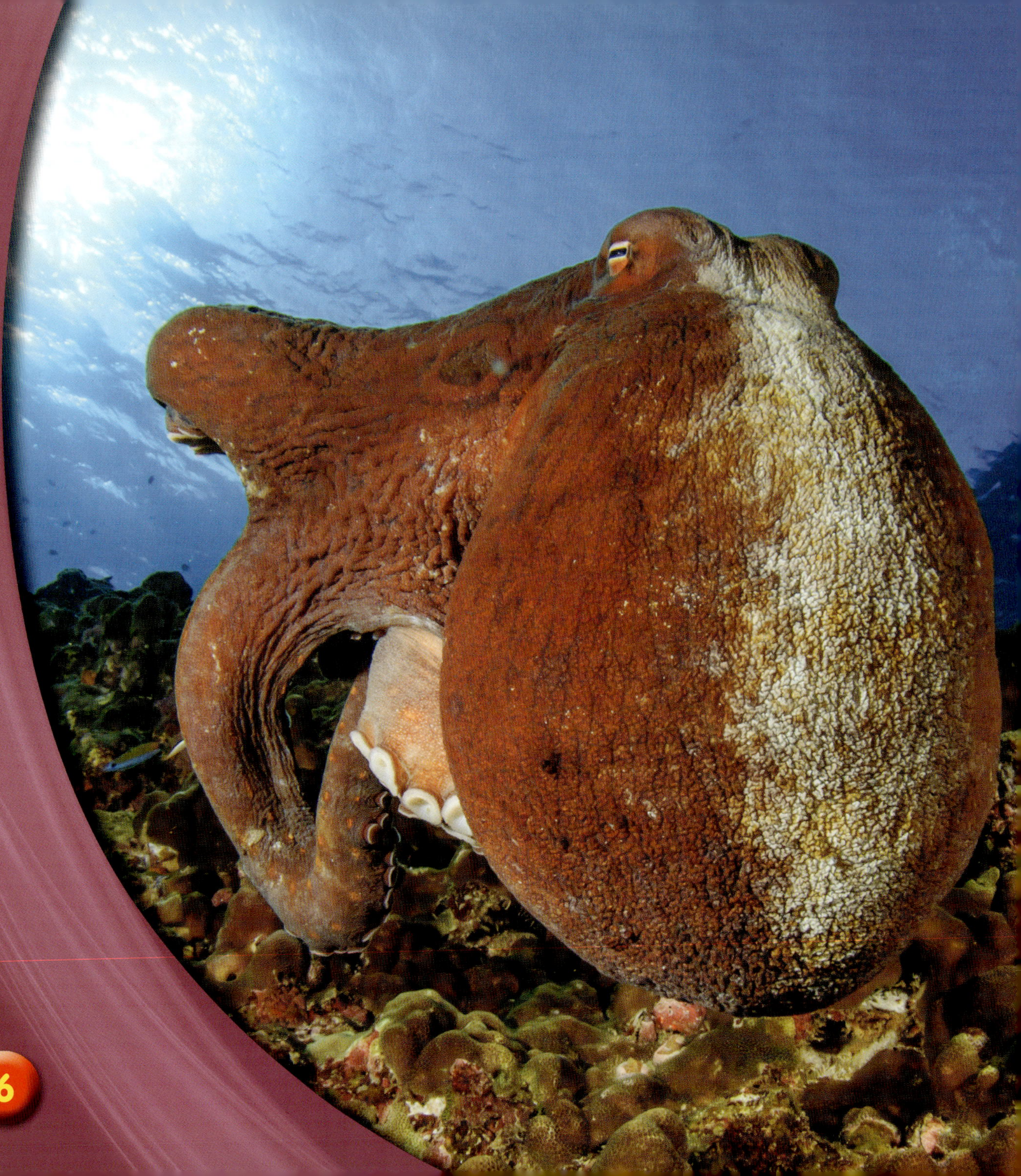

Octopuses do not look like any other animal. No other animal has a head, arms, and no other body parts! Its head is called a **mantle**.

Octopuses do not have any bones. Their only hard body part is their sharp beak.

This octopus has a very large mantle.

8

Octopuses live alone. Even though some are big, they can hide in a seashell or a coconut shell. Octopuses have a good memory. They can even open jars! They are curious but shy.

LOOK! Have you ever seen an octopus up close? Where did you see one? How did it move?

This octopus is hiding in a shell.

10

Octopuses Keep Safe

Octopuses have many ways to stay safe. They can change their color quickly. This is called **camouflage**.

This octopus likes to blend into its surroundings.

12

An octopus releases black ink when it is scared or hurt. The ink confuses a **predator**'s sense of smell. It irritates their eyes. That lets the octopus move to safety.

This octopus is releasing a black cloud of ink.

14

An octopus can hide in a small crack to keep safe. Predators swim by. They do not see the octopus.

This octopus is hiding in a coral reef. It lives off an island in California.

16

Octopuses can bite with their sharp beak. They can move fast. They swim headfirst. Their tentacles trail behind them. An octopus can also crawl along the ocean floor on two arms.

CREATE! List five interesting facts about octopuses. Share them with a friend.

Octopuses swim headfirst.

18

Looking at Tide Pools

Octopuses only live in ocean water. They live all over the world.

This octopus has crawled onto the beach.

20

Sometimes ocean water gets trapped in little holes in the beach. These pools of water are called **tide pools**.

Look in one closely. You might see an octopus!

This octopus from South Africa is in a tide pool.

Think About It

Octopuses are strong and can defend themselves, especially with their ink clouds. But they try to avoid other animals. Why do you think that is?

Ask your parents or teacher if you can visit an aquarium to see octopuses. Before you go, write down what you think you will see. When you return home, write down what you saw.

Sometimes people cook octopus tentacles to eat. Would you ever try a bite of one? Why or why not?

Find Out More

BOOK
Thomas, Elizabeth. *Octopuses*. Ann Arbor, MI: Cherry Lake Publishing, 2014.

WEB SITE
Smithsonian—Ten Curious Facts About Octopuses
www.smithsonianmag.com/science-nature/ten-curious-facts-about-octopuses-7625828/?no-ist
Read these 10 weird trivia facts about octopuses.

Glossary

camouflage (KAM-uh-flahzh) how an animal blends with its surroundings

mantle (MAN-tuhl) the head of an octopus

octo (AHK-toh) a prefix that means "eight"

predator (PRED-uh-tur) an animal that lives by hunting other animals to eat

tentacles (TEN-tuk-kuhlz) one of the long, flexible limbs of some animals that are used to move and to grasp things

tide pools (TIDE POOLZ) small pools of water by the ocean's shore that form when the tide is low

Index

appearance, 5, 7, 9, 11
arms, 5

beak, 7, 17
behavior, 9, 11, 13, 15, 17
bite, 17
bones, 7

camouflage, 11

habitat, 9, 15, 19, 21
humans, 22

ink, 13, 22

mantle, 7
memory, 9
movement, 17

octo, 5

predator, 13, 15
protection 11, 13, 15, 22

regeneration, 5

size, 9
swimming, 17

tentacles, 5, 17
tide pools, 19, 21

About the Author

Helen Foster James likes to read, travel, and hike in the mountains with her friends. She loves to see octopuses when she's snorkeling in California. She has traveled thousands of miles to see them in the tide pools in the Tuamotu Islands. She lives by the Pacific Ocean in San Diego, California, with her husband, Bob.